Acknowledgements

Some of these poems have appeared in the following magazines:

The Honest Ulsterman, The Spectator, Rhinoceros, Salmon, Cyphers, The Irish Times, The Belfast Newsletter, The Maryland Poetry Review, Poetry Ireland, Listen, The Irish Press, Poetry Review, Quarry, The Missouri Review, Gown (GLB), Grain and Westerly. I thank the editors for their encouragement. Earlier versions of two of these poems appeared in my selected *Poems 1956/86* published by Gallery Press, Ireland and Bloodaxe, England in 1986.

Since I retired from teaching in 1984 I have been helped to concentrate on writing by The Arts Council of Northern Ireland with a bursary, and later with their contribution to my stint as writer in residence at Queen's University, Belfast, where they taught me the use of the word processor, a machine exactly suited to poetic creation. Since then Aosdana's grants have helped me finish 'The Cattle Rustling' (Fortnight Publications, 1991), the newer poems in this collection and 'A Boyhood in the Colony,' an account of my first 17 years, which has yet to find a publisher.

'Sex, Rectitude and Loneliness' has been published separately as a pamphlet by Lapwing Press, Belfast.

Dedication

To Janice and Ben and Anna and in memory of my mother and my sister, Mary, who died in recent years.

'I ain't the doctor, and I ain't the doctor's son, but I'll stick with you, baby, till the doctor come.'

Janice

My love, my softy, my brown swan,
swimming now in the brimming river
of my affections. Will you swim on
forever and forever.

My love, my freckled gardener
busy with balm and briony,
Americanly kind and conscious
of the limitations of irony . . .

supportive to a fault, hurt
by local abrasiveness, our wit,
the winding up and putting down,
brilliance that has no heart in it.

I grow less Irish every year
with kindly love to lean upon.
Our home and garden is my nation,
my freckled gardener, my swan.

Contents

Beginning Again

In Society

Exploration in the Arts

Former Relationships

The African Poems

Beginning Again

Valentine for Ariadne
(whose silken thread led me out of it)

Here is my old man's love, serene and mild,
for your asthma-haunted body your bladder burning,
your collapsed lung, sick father, our stillborn child.
You watch the mirror for your shape returning,

but if we can never recover what used to be,
you're getting healthier daily, and content
already coddles us, you as you are and me.
We don't look back or ask what that darkness meant.

Your Valentine is delighted you're sane and just.
You'd rather I'd be jealous!
                                    I was, too,
for women who weren't one half as good as you.
The thrill in addictive love is the lack of trust.

We love our company . . . won't do without it . . .
not like relationships we had before.
Giving comes easily and will come more . . .
perhaps because we don't think much about it.

I've promised you another fifty years . . .
just the best brands of whiskey and cigarettes;
but if I do not much outlast my peers . . .
if Ben is thirty . . . we'll have no regrets.

We, in The Poets' House above the harbour,
greet the damp mildness of returning spring
with private jokes and undiminished ardour,
you at your stitching, I at my hoovering,

planting the absent oaks you advertise
in your Portmuck poem.

Calm yourself, James! Command
peace in your soul, pause, look in her eyes . . .
the shade the sea takes, shallow over sand.

New England self-improvers, we're in league.
The signs of love flash like a steady glow
at meals, at work, in sickness and fatigue,
in bed when Ben cries.

'OK Let *me* go,'

either might say, and both would calculate
who is too drunk or if it's you or me
most needs a rest.

Incomprehensible hate,
that scared us, roaring, like the Irish sea
night after night engulfing our harbour wall,
fell back this morning. It harmed nothing at all.

Elegy for a Deadborn Child

"Up stepped the cabin boy and bravely out spoke he.
He said to the captain, 'What will you give to me,
if I will swim alongside the Spanish enemy
and sink her in the lowlands lowlands low,
sink her in the lowland sea?'"
            The Golden Vanity.

1
A brief addition to the family
shown and withdrawn in the longest moment of my life.

All our concern was how to help my wife
endure and survive bearing a dead baby,
all that intrusion, bruising and abuse.

An Indian doctor told us the law said
she must be satisfied the child was dead
before the mother could be treated, induce
labour and get that clot of blood excreted,
remove what now we waited for with dread.

Most of the day we waited.

2
This morning was a holiday. After we woke
we made love. Then suddenly the waters broke.
There should be absolutely no connection
all the doctors insisted. However you thrust
up the vagina the hardest erection
it never troubles the small life held in trust.

The waters broke. The mildest irritation
of wet sheets, and slowly the implication.
The ignorant husband had to be told no embryo
survives the drying up of the amniotic sea.
She gradually brought it home to me.
I had plans for the morning that I must forego.

3

Different doctors on duty had different views,
the nurses made sour faces. It was easy to lose
track. Experts don't always want to say
what they know. Patients are at their mercy.
A corpse in the womb is suddenly dangerous.
The mother is naturally loathe to make a fuss,

pretty and clean in her cotton shift, her mind
grinding to grasp problems, her nerves strained.

Then they came in to inject her. They wheeled her away,
me following, then banished, then restored. I had no say.

'You're doing great, dear,' said a coarse
assistant. 'Push down, hard, to your arse.
Lovely. Push down again, like a hard shit.'

So gods are born. She was glad to be rid of it.

That mind, that body tests the hospital,
nurses and surgeons. In her, nature is ill.
Even the architect, the administration
bear down on her, their skill and limitation.
Nature is fighting nature, their illness fights
her illness. The woman bleeds under the lights.

4

Four inches long, on folded cotton wool
whatever it was lay,
fleshy, like a pork fillet on a butcher's tray,
skin that transparent,
and he pointedly wasn't looking at you,
exact and remote, a small bronze statue.

Closer, his big head was shapely, one arm
folded across a wren-bone chest,
the tiny hands poised, halted
in some activity. No harm
had come to the long fingers; but he was dead.
The little cabin boy had done his best.

We were learning him, like our other little one.
He was him in miniature, and Ben is small enough.
A brother then, somebody worth mourning.
Mother and father released at last from the rough
mismanagement of hospitals, learning
a sense of loss and reward, to love their son.

5

As we looked and touched
questions were put to us
by nurse and doctor,
how to dispose of this?

To us, tragic and rarely:
to them, unfortunate but daily.
Us, shocked, inclined to hurt,
but resentment was silly.

We could take the thing home,
make of our garden
a private graveyard
with a single headstone,

or make his bed under the roses
or store his ashes in vases,
or leave him lying
where the admin disposes.

Not home surely!
Our bad dog, Charlie,
would smell out meat
and resurrect him early.

We were hard put to decide,
until formaldehyde
the preserver was suggested.
That left us goggle-eyed.

Let the administrator
dispose of the little creature
in whatever usual way,
dustbin or incinerator.

Only in heart and memory
let him survive. Bury him
silent, invisible,
within us, without ceremony.

6
I always hated magic.
I lost Jesus for that.
Let happen whatever happens,
let the dead lie
stinking of death and life,
finished, flat.
Let all who knew him
exercise memory.
To be born dead

is to be wondered at,
and I wonder.
No one is going to cry.
The wake
will be very private.

7
Released at last
from that stark theatre,
the steel bowls and blood,
the bleak unhomeliness,
a warehouse, an empty supermarket,

I wheeled you back
to the private bedroom,
its high windows brimming
with green blue sky
of gorgeous evening
after the long day.

We could lie together,
the bruised, bereaved mother,
and her tired lover, semi-conscious
of a pelmet of wispy clouds
being drawn across
the glowing shell of moon.

We were part of the long hot summer of '89
again,
      exiled in Belfast's Royal Hospital
from our new home by the sea,

                              everything
bad happening and never happier.

                                    My mother
was half a mile away,

                        down in the City,

slowly and unreluctantly
loosing her tough old
hold on life.

8
I drifted back in history,
living another blazing summer,
relished in Donegal
with a different cast
of loved ones, lost now,

one who went off
to England – no bother –
for an abortion
and returned smiling.
She said, 'The day after
we walked down to the station,
three girls with our wee cases.
It was a holiday.'

9

Janice, you've heard me calling Ben
Charlie, the dog's name, when
I was tired. And Anna, it's well known,
I call by the names of children
with children of their own,
so separate lives get mixed and blend,
Ben and our dead embryo, Helen and Anna.
I like that mystic feel. I cry 'Hosannah'
for birth, for parenthood. Can you let me say,
'Anna is Rachael is Helen is Penelope?'
And I've called you by the names of previous wives,
shuffling my past and duplicating lives.
I stand by this: my mother did the same.
Don't think these quirks insulting or inane,
I was my father, Stewart, to her or my nephew,
Michael, males who at different times she knew
by the one tie of her love, for eternity,
petering out now in Ward 23
in stray smiles, as her mind holds or slips.
I consult my watch, and kiss her withered lips.
Love is confusing, in the surge and relapse
we all fill gaps in other lives and leave gaps
to be filled. Leave my mistakes uncorrected.
In confusion the lost lovers are less neglected.
And if you start calling me Don Paul after
your Scottish lover, promise each other laughter
not hurt, embarrassment or accusation.
Bow to the good times. Honour collaboration.

10

Your eyes closed. When your breath was regular
I walked alone down long bright corridors,
unlocked our battered Peugeot and drove home.
Somewhere along the way I stopped involuntarily,
maybe exhausted, and slumped over the wheel,
embracing an old friend who always starts
in the morning and takes us where we have to go.
The son and sister I am driving to
will wait. I sensed above me, above the city
up in the evening sky, something going home,
like one of the lighter planes you see lose height,
down, out of sight, to the harbour. This was my own
son, a failed impulse from the teeming earth
returned, too little, and too lately known.

"His mates they dragged him up, and on the deck he died.
They sewed him in his hammock that was so fair and wide,
then they lowered him overboard and he's drifting with the tide,
drifting in the lowlands, lowlands low,
drifting in the lowland sea."

When Ben was Ill in Hospital

1

'Egnell: lacte amida'

She would express herself three times a day.
They taught my girl, his mother, the proper way
to use the square machine that sang and breathed
quietly, and her swollen breasts relieved.
Lacte Amida extracted milk by suction,
making our bed a milking parlour. The action
was painless and pleasant. It worked perfectly,
this box inspired by electricity.
I was hypnotised by the metal cylinder swinging
a few inches backwards and forwards, singing.
At the end of a tube was the plastic funnel she pressed,
alternately, ten minutes at each breast.
The machine whirred like a little factory
plonked on our duvet, pleasantly working away.
Her brown nipples were drawn nearly an inch
into a vacuum; but this was a cinch
compared to other tasks they gave us, waiting,
helpless, while surgeons were operating.
Egnell was a gentle seducer, with no fuss
using her breasts for Ben. Could I be jealous?

2

'Egnell: lacte amida' was not our own,
we only had it a few weeks on loan
from the hospital. A more deserving case
required it. A nameless gadget took its place,
worked manually. Our fingers had to squeeze
a rubber bulb. There was no more lying at ease
being milked. This was a helper we ended hating.
It was hard work and even humiliating

for it looked like an old car horn, comic at best,
a honker that had no right to your breast,
neither effective nor companionable.
And in the end the doctors were unable
to use the little bottles you and I
filled up so patiently, and your breasts went dry.

3

Janice, that time we had to trust machines
to keep Ben breathing. Hope was in plastic lines
that fed him milk and vitamins, tubes that could suck
mucus from his clogged throat. Neither love nor luck
kept Ben among us where he is today,
it was harsh experts and scalpel and X-ray.
Cutting his flesh, breaking his rib was smart,
detaching his wandering throat from his tiny heart.
We were spectators; but the little shit
was as tough as they were, fighting out the bit
like a warrior, enduring the sore cuts,
surviving, angry and helpless. It took guts
and a sound heart; but the tubes that kept him going
he tried to tear out recklessly, unknowing
they forced life on him, more than he could bear.
He preferred death to discomfort, but they held him there.

Your hands and mine could touch his spindly thighs
among the needles, mourn for his bruised eyes.
A long time in that clean well-lighted place
we watched his stubborn head and chubby face,
blue eyes and small hard chin, much like my own,
familiar from father and mirror. I have known
Ben's face for a lifetime. Here he belongs,
with us who stroked his head and sang him songs.

Honeymoon in Greece

A wholesome milkmaid is my darling,
salesgirl for Camembert or Brie,
fresh with desire, like many milkmaids,
not for the world at large but me.

Her clothes are neat and even swanky,
designer dresses are her style
and family jewels, yet hanky panky
is in her repertoire, and guile.

Speaker of ancient Greek, this scholar
walks on the wild side. Local prigs
call her a filthy Yankee hooer;
she shouts, 'Your grannies all fucked pigs.'

I am the trembling male protector.
'Might they come back?' she queries. 'Yes!'
In crises I turn tail, like Hector;
but still, like Hector, I impress.

The rude Greeks ride off out of ear shot.
Unlike dogs they can't smell my fear.
I stand erect, five feet eleven,
glaring until they disappear.

My stature often must have saved me,
making my long life trouble free.
Now I lie down beside my woman,
admitting fear heroically,

enjoying her learning, easy-carried
her silk chemise, her Paris hat.
She mocks my vulgar quizzing habit
of quoting poems, then, 'Who wrote that?'

A soft breeze stirs our summer clothing.
(Into my heart an air that killed?)
Nothing is irritating, boring.
We don't admit being slightly chilled.

This is the holiday of marriage
on shore again in sweet relief.
Respite is just as real as danger,
though mostly time brings love to grief.

The Rainbow

Riding forward in love, youth facing age,
they reclined in a dirty Ulster railway carriage.
The wide-screen window panoramically
displayed North Antrim towards the hills and sea,
like an actress doing her fabulous routine,
a lovely fascinating old has-been.
The foreground whipped past: hedges, embankments, cows
in sloping fields, a prosperous farm house,
towns, Antrim, Ballymena, angled streets,
rivers, a round tower, scenes of the feats
performed over forty years from youth to age.
They drank her welcome to his heritage
of grey, grey-green, wet earth and shapes of stone.
Who weds a landscape will not die alone.

This was his railway, Derry to Belfast.
The new young wife beside him felt his past
travelling with them, flying and in pursuit.
Adventuring again, he felt her foot
toying with his foot till his eye caught her eye.
As empty cans of Fanta rattled by
on the filthy floor, they left their drab seats singly
and met in the cramped toilet, untousled, tingly
with anticipation. He watched her hoist herself
with casual elegance up on a handy shelf
made by the wash-basin and window ledge.
Her right leg, green silk clad, became a wedge
closing the ruined door. In her mink coat
she was the mountaineer who found a route
to the fabulous summit, her skirt above her thighs,
her face dipping towards him while his eyes
feasted on the curly, tangled pubic hair
moist on her steaming nether lips, and there

his penis, stiff and rosy, was now aimed.
She had lost her panties, so her cunt was framed
by the frilly corset ridge and cute suspenders,
as though to advertise a home for members,
a summer palace standing without sentry.
He rose up on his toes for easier entry,
between those white thighs in their silken hose,
to the softest spongiest welcome a man knows.
She groaned and sighed and whispered something rude,
the pure essential sound of gratitude.
He unbuttoned the blouse under her flowing coat
to free her breasts her shoulders and her throat
which must be kissed. The swaying of the train
helped him to come as she came once again.
They reached down for the magnum of champagne
cooled in the toilet, wrapped in cellophane.

They were back in their seats by Ballymoney. His life
had seemed to stop there when his second wife
died; but now drunk with their hilarious
success, 'God, show us what you think of us!'
he shouted, and saw, out of this soaking arable
countryside rise up a parable,
a pure electric rainbow in the fog,
bright colours like a painter's catalogue,
orange, magenta, red, indigo violet,
towering and curving, huge, immaculate,
unbent, unblurred from weightless foot to foot,
a flowering arch from what miraculous root?
Light-hearted, sated, stilled, these lovers knew
a gate had opened and they both passed through.

Janice and Me
(a song)

We're virtuous.
New books on how to live refer to us.
We're mild and funny and so courteous,
why do they wish us gone.

We're civilised.
Apprentice gurus would be well advised
to watch us closely as we shine and rise,
equal to dusk and dawn.

Blue skies
shine up above us
every room has a view.
Her eyes
are always shining.
She says
mine are too.

We're virtuous.
In tribulation we don't make a fuss.
Why can't you other people be like us,
talented, wise and true?

It must be awful to be you.

Or are you virtuous too?
Will books on how to live refer to you?
Are you much different, but still good and true.
Tell me, and I'll tell you . . .
'The humble always muddle through.'

The Last Supper
for Desmond Maxwell

Stoven on Thursday with Dessy and NA.
Can't function by 9 pm. Bed.
Not wicked and wasteful. OK.

Awake on Friday, wishing to be dead;
but tea and aspirins . . . What did we say?
We chatted of old times. Remember Dessy said

he dreamed of having a great party
for the living remains of his acquaintance
world wide. Friendship is here to stay!

I think his idea makes sense,
and he has the money to bring
his whole past into the present tense.

I couldn't do it. I chose to sing
notes more and more exalted, leaving
behind those who were faltering.

Dessy, you never cared a toss
for your scholarship. It only earned
you a good living that appeased the loss

of Derry for a while; but you always burned
to have it again. You only made new friends
who would please those you never spurned

or neglected. Early on progress ended.
After that first apotheosis of learning to smoke –
of drink, poetry, friendship – everything tended

to barbarity: Presley for Al Bowly,
Russ Conway for Fats Waller, anyone recent
for TS Eliot, the trendy replacing the holy . . .

for talent is holy and friendly we would say,
like Dickinson of Leeds on mountaineers,
'a chosen sect throwing their lives away'.

You have worn yourself out with friendship to a holy ghost
blindly arranging a final supper for all
your living and dead, my friend, mine host.

A Sort of Prospero

Their gossip cut me from my audience,
prevented public practice of my arts.
My power was only over minds and hearts
earned by the tactless truths I could dispense.

Fastidious, frightened . . . not my finest hour;
but I had wife and children and my art
to cherish. Our belongings in a cart,
we left the city to those who craved for power.

I say they drove me out – that is to say
my privateness, morality and skill
reproached my peers – became political.
I didn't stay and fight; I sailed away . . .

and shipwrecked on this island, back to old haunts
of nature . . . déjà vu . . . but, 'Oh, what larks!'
What space and stillness after public parks
and teeming streets and clamorous restaurants.

I wake to clouds and islands at their stations
on still bright mornings in the garden, feeding
the donkey docken and scutchgrass from my weeding,
planting out mallow, cranesbill and carnations.

Our Caliban is a woman, husband dead,
drowned. She needs cash, is good at everything,
cleaning and setting fires and gossiping.
My Ariel came with me in my head.

What are we waiting for? Wages of sin?
To see usurpers washed up on our shores,
the corrupt brokers and scared servitors,
quaking, our former creatures and our kin

skulking among these hills and hedges? Repent!
Cringing by primroses that each spring grow
on the third hill's corner? Damn it, No!
Let them discover their own punishment,

eating each other, as they will, no doubt,
as 'cruel' burns through the frail mask of 'witty'
at New Year's party or high-powered committee.
Our best of magic is to keep them out.

Intrusions on the Idyll

The cry of seagulls half a mile away
under the soaring skies I loved before
under duress on a far different shore,
echo in our front garden on a quiet day.

Beautiful masks – our island with its thirty
shades of green, its browns, its sunset gold:
the rat holes, corpses, shrieking gulls, bones, old
combative nature, hungry, angry, dirty.

Nature? The nature of life to be dual;
hospitable, voluble, musical . . . and superstitious;
slow, enduring, intelligent . . . and vicious.
I hear the cries of my people, wrong and cruel.

So are the English. So are we all. The lights
of home draw us, smiling, to the green and pleasant
land, the barren high bog, the picturesque peasant,
bowing to clergy, voting for ignorant shites.

Birds

Now we make carefree forays to Belfast
and drive our car back up the sloping lane
on a surge of joy, of coming home again,
in second or third gear, and a huge cast

of whatever tiny elegant fowl, that fly
ahead as harbingers between the hedges,
blithely evades our cutting, thrusting edges,
the passage of a happy family.

What is a bird's life like? Too hard to say.
Like the leper beggar children in Africa
waving their stumps, and us going 'ha ha ha'
at repartee, relaxed deformity.

With measured speech, safe home and innocent,
a formula that James Joyce didn't try,
we've gambled on the country, she and I.
Can one be happy and still relevant?

Ben's at my elbow, breathing in the ashes
from my foul ashtray. These, he says, are eggs,
this bowl of apples. His fingers make the legs
of an imaginary bird. His long lashes

and his small handsome face live in the corner
of my busy eye, inventing, inventing. There,
we are eating the apple, and giving the bird share.
I would invent half rhymes, bring on the farmer . . .

but my wife calls out from the kitchen to reach her down
platters she cannot reach, to serve us all.
I should have held out for one six feet tall;
but I help her, without complaint, and then bend down

and kiss her sweetly and long, and suddenly feel
as beautiful myself as birds, and laugh
at my brilliant, blonde and glowing better half
who loves me for my virtues which are real.

Charlie

Charlie, they bought me you for Fathers' Day

Now you are nearly the old woman of the sea,
neutered before you ever accomplished sex,
you only tried out vaguely on the cats,
persistently but gentlemanly.

Your bark says, 'Better to marry than to burn.'

We think of you as a loving old silly,
whining when we leave, leaping up on our return,
stone chaser and chewer, football burster.
I regret not being a bird hunter or a gillie
who would put you to clever use and teach
you skills. We throw stones for you on the beach,
and tease and stroke and cuddle you a lot.

This is a nice wild area and you wander free.

It is better to be neutered than be shot,
we said yesterday when you bit our neighbour.
It was one too many bites. We can't construe
your angers and we can't speak to you.
You always go for the postman, once our
friend, your teeth bared horribly, leaping
at his rapidly closing window. His frightened face
grown ugly. Maybe he kicked you, we speculate;
but I've kicked you to put you in your place.
You don't hate me. Is it red cars you hate?

You behave badly, and you are in our keeping.

You bark for any arrival day or night,
people or cars; but the moment they're entered
and at home you fawn and lick their hands . . .
with one exception, the small bad tempered
farmer, nipped in the hall, and nip is bite.
We can't talk grandly of keeping off our lands
the interlopers. We don't want to. We want
your company, but human flesh is sacrosanct.

'Get that mongrel away from my sheep,' he shouted,
'or I'll shoot him.' And he was right, Ned,
a pregnant sheep is an investment. We didn't parley;
but you're cured of sheep-chasing this long
time. The neighbours know and love 'Charlie'.
Everyone rolls your fine name on his tongue
and smiles . . . except the postman and the milkman
and the odd dandering city clan
of holiday children you sometimes terrify,
leaping over the back wall to the lane.

The noble profile poised at window sills,
our bonehead mongrel of the Baskervilles.

It was one too many you nipped with Mrs Hatrick
who drove back promptly and showed her shapely leg
with marks of teeth no friendly licking will lick
off. She said, nicely, she wasn't complaining,
she knew you weren't a bad dog. She was meaning
that country life is harsh . . . no need to beg
forgiveness; but she needed a tetanus jag.

We knew someone was going to report you, you clown,
sooner or later. And then you'd be put down.

I rang the vet, who was civil and couldn't be sure,
but neutering was a high percentage cure
for excitable dogs. It cost £47.

We have no lead. I whistled you in and left.

That evening it seemed I felt your absence more
than I ever felt your presence, as a hollow
behind my legs, for up and down you follow
around the house. When I'm at stool you scratch
the door, or burst in if its off the latch.
When I went to bed and slept I was still bereft,
your black shadow was absent from the floor.

Next day the nice girl carried you out to the car
with this plastic lampshade round your neck
to keep your teeth from where the stitches are,
and all this week around the house you knock
on door jambs and rattle like a shelf
of tin mugs when you scratch yourself.

You look up with your perfect grizzled head,
a sable silvered, a Dutch portrait with elaborate
ruff, dignified as any burgher. I wrote,
'dognified.' My daughter might well hate
a father who does such things. And Wendy said
her father had tied a dead hen round the neck
of his dog to cure his killing habit. Heck,
I can't tie a postman round you! He's not dead.

Before I hear, you hear his van, and the low groan
starts in your throat. Charlie, you aren't cured yet;
but, 'It may take weeks for every aggressive hormone
to work its way out of the system,' said the vet.

My wife was the one who knew this would set you free.
If I bite her she'll do the same for me.

Sestina of the Seaboard

The nylon rope slapping the metal mast,
a forest clapping coldly in the dark,
and I alone unsleeping, close to the roof.
No other vessel had a man on board.
The small yacht strained against the mooring rope.
'Rangoon by morning!' Captain Billy cried.

'The rising sea's too much for me,' I cried.
Fear and mistakes. There was the broken mast
and only Billy who could climb the rope –
his competence a beacon in our dark.
Two assholes and a sailor were aboard.
He climbed into our swaying shattered roof.

Nerve was like metaphysics. We called roof
what was beyond us as we whinged and cried,
keen but incompetent to be aboard
so thin a vessel with so high a mast
that in full daylight left us in the dark,
two lubbers with a slack and useless rope,

in crisis lost, though smart enough with rope
in light winds. Now I feel the shallow roof
press on my head. I feel the lonely dark.
When she went off with someone else I cried
and felt no seaman's feeling for the mast
we all gazed up to as we came aboard.

Aboard, ashore, aboard, ashore, aboard.
You buy a boat and tie it with a rope.
You look up scared by far too high a mast,
but sleep well underneath the lowly roof.
And even Captain Billy might have cried
alone in the small cabin in the dark.

A boat is for exploring. Moored in the dark,
with no companions, the one man aboard,
I cried alone, and many would have cried.
Don't hang us from the yard arm by a rope
who should have stuck beneath our family roof
now and before . . . frightened to climb a mast,

to climb a cross in darkness, the high mast.
They hacked at the boarded windows, the thatched roof.
Crying, we felt them hack home's last straw rope.

Outing to Port a doris

There is an old faint path to Port a doris,
once you've been shown
that curved iron swing-gate stile,
peculiar to Inishowen,
beside the gate proper for carts, cattle
and cultivation.
Our path is worn by trim shoes on picnics
for generations,
not farmers. This is a middle-class quest
for beauty in the wilderness
of these small bays, useless for boats,
just rocky promontories
poking the Atlantic ocean, placid today,
the tide slopping in almost silently.
I am the stiff old guide now who was once
child of the picnic parties,
headlong and curious, ferns above my head,
in the early forties.
Our generations never found trace of others
on the faint track.
We thought only our friends and families
had kept the brambles back.
McRitchie, Kelso, Montgomery,
Stinson, Wright, treading the way.

Today we follow the edge of the oatfield, straying
among bright green shoots
from the faint path only where the stream has spilled
over and wets our boots;
then, at last, to remembered rocks and white
sand and marram grass
under the drizzle of an Irish July. I point
our little party past

ferns and briars up steep and narrow ways
from one secret bay
and down again to the next, farther and farther
from huckster-shop holidays.

I am Ben's father. He's the boy quirky with life.
David and Eloise are friends, Janice, my wife.
We gaze at the final long promontory
over the fourth ridge,
advancing towards it, tired, anticipatory.
Under my eyelids
images crush from past times, past
but still alive,
faces on the quest still, eager, uncertain,
demanding love,

a crowd that confronts and follows me over the new
rock fall. These ancient
forms shift and disintegrate! We are through
the cave-like entrance
to our small hidden beach, its lofty walls,
precipitous stony face.
In barren spaces above us wiry sheep
tear at the wild grass.

The stones we came for are medium to minuscule,
but not yet sand,
still being ground down. I am down, kneeling,
scooping with my hand
this pure jewellery, looking for something for her,
under this soft
rain and light. We crowd this precious carpet,
kneeling down to sift
treasure, hands rinsing stones
through to gravel.

I have told them here is the one place I know
to find a cowrie shell.

The four year old is in his element,
fighting smooth rocks that look
like beasts, like people turned to stone.
It is out of a story book.
I, the magician of picnics, light a fire
with a tissue and driftwood.
We are all happy and glad to be here;
but if I only could
find my woman the once and future gift
of that shell . . .
if my generations have left one . . . they are rare
and therefore spiritual,

the tiny cunty under part, and the curling
pink ribbed back. Here! 'Here it is, darling.'

Brown's Bay, Sunday, October

The shore looked cold, dark and forbidding,
but it was mild enough in the car park.
High seas, hardly noticed, had remodelled
the shore the family played on last Sunday,
black with sea wrack ripped from the sea's bed,
black as Ben's incongruous cowboy hat
under which he explored the edges of the stream,
his wide Missouri, jungles, deserts, hills.

Anna, at nine, was closer to me, testing
her nerve and skill on stepping stones. Ben,
four, was absorbed by everything. Indoors
he needed others; 'Help me to build this castle.'
When you moved the first Lego brick
and failed to complete his imagined castle
he complained, a tiny enigmatic dictator.
Here, in nature, he didn't need our services.
The sand, malleable, markable, unbreakable,
the spectacle of fiercely running water,
enthralled him. Not, seemingly, adventurous,
he drew what looked like A with his plastic knife.
I made it A B C with the metal spade.
His toe rejected pedagogy.

I withdrew into myself into the car.
Before I settled to the intricate sports pages
my eyes lifted to ocean, dark green further out,
and in, where the waves broke, the foam was dark,
a luminous grey almost, like the world
through dark glasses. The waves were mauve
the shade latent in wild blackberries.

When the sun is bright like this, slanting
from Shane's hill, the three aquiline headlands
recede in fainter shades of grey, an autumn seascape.
It has all happened before. Families
before my families on well known beaches
blessed by sunlight before the last war
or the next, mingle their shouts and silences
with ours. A good woman has walked out of sight
with one of the children down the long strand,
and when I edge stiffly out of the driver's seat
and fold the newspaper, no one is going to complain.
The children are ready to go home for tea,
and, walking back content, her gesture to me,
that feels like absolution, is casual, friendly.

Aphrodite

We call this Aphrodite's Place
for here she would laze
on the grassy heights, delighted
at the suddenly wine-dark sea.

On those residential days
fishermen passed below us blithely
seeing what were usually lethal currents
made harmless by her gaze.

Ballycastle
for Medbh

I once came down here with Ernie Mann's 'Black
Songbirds,' after dark, from Portrush, this town's
big sister up the coast that lies on her stiff back,
open, exposed . . . houses built on a spine of rock
sticking out, looking down on the broad
Atlantic, sharp like a bird's beaked head . . .
Portrush is not dead stone, it shouts and sings,
leaning back, always. I remember the beaches flowed
whitely from her shoulders like stretched wings.

Everything shelters Ballycastle and looks down . . .
the wooded hills and headlands. Driving here,
in daylight, you descend the glen by stages – three
spangled green tunnels of old trees – and suddenly
drop into the sheltered heart of the town,
down a hill of pubs, grocers and hardware
to the spired Anglican church, the market square.

I never looked till today – but it *is*
a market town with houses for families,
butchers, chemists, a substantial Catholic school
under the comforting, curved and nippled
grey breast of Knoclaide – the broad hill
I climbed with my first wife one crucial
fair day, when noise and pleasure rippled.

Boys from Portrush came down to the Royal Hotel
on Sunday nights for dances to raise hell
in a small way. Today I followed the one street down
out of the town centre to the sea: all
the gardens have high thick hedges crowned
with roses, safe houses for retirement, and space
for gapped ruins rented by trees and grass.

The countryside comes right down to the shore
to tennis, contested on top of the Dane's harbour,
the kept turf of the golf course that surrounds
the Priory. Herbs, crushed by our spiked shoes
in the springy grass, raise perfumes that confound
our senses like turf smoke and seagull cries.
Council improvement teams obscure the views.
. . . .

Glen's foot and river's end –
the curved shore is sheltered
by might headlands.
Under the cliffs, Medbh's house nestles,
Not far out, but all alone,
in the sea's mouth broad Rathlin
is the big stone.

In Society

Drinking Under Margaret Thatcher

We never were worse off, so short
it's often not up to ourselves
that we're having one snort
too little. Empty pockets. Empty shelves.

But the overdraft can usually stand
one more bottle. And if the hole in the wall
denies you, there's always some friend
who'll know why you've come to call.

There's little joy in not earning,
less in being totally skint,
none to think of yourself learning
better habits from that bint.

War on Want

1

In these days of touch and go
you have more grandchildren than you suppose.
A thin boy in the War on Want
shop has the family nose.
Wedged at his shabby granny's knee
he is shaking his head against her gross
mortifying bribery: 'Will ye not go
for a run to the Port with your granda?' Me.
'Will ye go to eat cake at the University?'

My son can hardly have been fourteen
when late one night I looked in
on his mountain eyrie. He was at the stage
of fixing padlocks on his door. The walls glistened
with black paint. Blown up grotesques
leered down from everywhere. I listened
for his breathing and heard breathing of two.
Asleep beside him was a blonde girl,
both fully dressed. How quickly they grew
up in those troubled times. We were not the best
of examples, my wife and I. Let the girl rest.
I lifted him under my arm, easily,
gently, warm as toast. Surely my one
hope was to hear nothing they had to say.
I bore him to another room stealthily.

Aware of them both sleeping floors above
I smoked and drank to my heart's content in the kitchen,
smiling and singing alone, like someone in love.

2

My son's coarse grained companion
and my wife took the same view. The bitch
certainly slept with everyone

and she certainly knew a soft touch
when she saw one. 'She's very fly
though she looks simple enough. She saw him coming!
Like son, like father.' I asked why?
'You're both soft touches with a taste for slumming.'

A soft touch, slumming. I had to call
at the cramped house in Killowen estate
where the mother was philosophical
and the girl was content it was too late
for argument. Her apron high by then,
she had only ever slept with the one,
she said, and, when I tried to explain,
she wouldn't hear of an abortion.

Sipping tea I heard myself offering
help, vaguely, financial aid
if they needed it, admitting nothing.
They didn't seem to be interested.
Flowers to the nursing home debacle,
and phoney high spirits! But, of course,
the baby was lovely, a miracle,
and the simple girl's tired face.

She found rearing children boring
though bearing them was no bother.
We heard she married and had more.
I met her twice somewhere or other.
My first grandson, if that was he,
seemed to stay mostly with his granny.
I called on him occasionally
in the dark shop, till we moved away.

3
Some nights, after a few whiskeys
I think grandly of making my will
if ever I hit the jackpot. I'll see
young whatshisname is comfortable.

Thompson the Gambler

'Would you call him a failed man, Tommy?' I was curious
about this spruce card player who, in middle age,
made crazy jokes when the play was fast and furious
and sometimes won, but was never centre stage.

'Thompson a failure? No. He has great respect.
There was never a better, though he's not good to the wife.
Did ye never hear of his big win? Homes were wrecked!
Money passed hands that night would keep us for life!'

'Is he rich, then?' 'No, not now. Can you understand,
he seemed to dislike the feel of having money.
He played like a fool, and he bought things out of hand:
a race-horse, a Rolls, drinks on the house. It was funny,

for it wasn't display. There was no one he'd care to impress.
He had to lose it to feel any sort of content.
If you haven't the hunger to win you enjoy cards less.
He went back to his old beginnings where he hadn't a cent.'

'And then he got hungry again? The hungry fighter?'
'Well, that was the trouble, he didn't. He could never forget
he had done it! I think you could say his heart is lighter,
he pays his way and he still loves cards, and yet,

good as he is, you'd never back him to win.
It was me that emptied ashtrays on his glory night.
When he'd done it, I pulled the curtains. The sun flowed in
and drained away the harshness of electric light

from cards, hard faces, soft money, from the war he'd won.
It's like war, a disciplined madness, a poker school.
They smoked and drank their whiskey and stared at the sun
on the rocks and the sea beyond. It was beautiful!'

My Father

I dreamed I saw my father as in life.
He burst in, angry, as he'd often done
shouting abuse at me and his tired wife
for ruining the hotel he had to run.

Old softy smiled her welcome. I knew
he was dead and buried, and yet there was such
reality in the dream I wept. Father withdrew
as always, not hostile, but hard to touch.

He gave his usual abrupt advice.
'Simmer and Jacks' was certainly the best buy
on the current market at the going price.
My dreams are silly, Mammy and Daddy and I

were met in a small pantry of our hotel,
hard drinkers and pretty girls sliding
up and down the stairs, police in the hall,
taking names. We, the owners, in hiding.

I was eager for revelation, but I was learning
nothing I didn't know. When his time was up,
his mouth began to fray, silently churning
like a worn rug, or a fag in a wet cup.

He held his hands to his mouth. My nerve broke
as he dissolved in pain . . . and I awoke.

The Guinness Spot

After the Scottish jazz singer in the Festival barn
I come on some lost acquaintances, willing to yarn
as though we had never lost touch. Disintegrated
dark holes in my life suddenly illuminated,
banging on brightly like pin-table lights.
It's a round table, and here's reunion of knights!

'You remember George Acheson, from Derry?'
He was jigging in offshore dusk like a night ferry,
a youth I know disguised as General Custer,
skinny and bearded and shaking my hand to muster
a warm response for someone he'd maybe rather
forget. He looks old enough to be my father.

He was one of a teenage bunch, a nice lot
humming like bees round my sister's honeypot,
all different, but all droll and seeming sure
of themselves. I thought I would never be so mature,
admiring their cheek and their wit and horse-play,
turning up at our door at dusk mysteriously.

And now his peculiar nasal drawl is approving
a bit of my prose remembering Derry with the loving
fascination of a child . . . days when the war
was ending. My heart's delighted, for he is a part
of a past I took to be dead. And here they are,
alive and kicking without the aid of art.

Paradise Enough

On the slow train from Glasgow to Stranraer
outside the window of the dining car
visions again. This pale sun has no trouble
releasing in fleeces of sheep a holy white
and tinting pink beneath them the furry stubble.
The sky is an arched cathedral of light.
The pale brown, leafless trees are glowing and group
elegantly, and a farmer with a thinker's stoop
stepping the crest of this hill field has slanted
his furrows in perfect symmetrical subtle curves,
taking his time to do what was clearly wanted.
Is my half smile what all of this deserves?

Now they are putting aureoles on cattle,
setting them near the skyline with winter sun
behind. A world of hymn subjects to one
brought up on hymns and a painting by Samuel Palmer
engraved on his mind. We are as cattle. From earth
we come, fiercely, to earth return, calmer.
No mean feat. Carriages rattle
and bump us along the calm Clyde's Firth.

For Conor Maguire's Christening
dedicated to Dr Anne Doherty

We're lucky your mother is here to hold you,
Conor, today at your christening.
I've written this out in verse to be told you
when you are fit for listening.

They tell me your birth went beautifully.
The nurses and doctors were full of praise.
And then you came home, content, you three,
enjoying these long bright summer days.

But one morning your mother's sheets were bright
with her own blood, a wombspill.
She had nursed. She knew enough to be frightened
and call for help. She was very ill.

The doctor, in tones of common sense,
said nothing was urgent. His telephone call
ordered the ordinary ambulance
and picked an unsuitable hospital.

It is worse for healers to be unskilled
than for most of us. They gave her water
when she needed blood, and nearly killed
your mother, Conor, and my daughter.

It is much for people to own their error
and seek advice when they are in doubt.
In time she was headed for Londonderry;
but time very quickly was running out.

And still she was misdirected, delayed
in the hospital corridors, till one
good doctor saw her and interfered
and insisted on treatment and saw it done.

Penelope's face is lovely above you,
the brighter because of the dark of danger.
Now she is safely here to love you
we are more inclined to relief than anger;

but we don't forget, and we dedicate
ourselves to living a better way –
strong-willed, concerned and accurate –
like that good physician, Anne Doherty.

Capital Punishment: USA

David Livingston Funchess
's life was reckoned a success
until Vietnam. The war he hated
left him much scarred and decorated,
five commendations, a Purple Heart.
A landmine blew his jeep apart;
that blew his mind. He couldn't cope.

The local hard drugs offered hope
of blurring all that fright and pain:
kind heroin and kind cocaine,
blankness at moonrise, darkness at noon.

'He came back crazy as a loon,'
says Veteran for Peace, Tom Fisher.
That's true. We have it from his sister
he worked the well known shell-shock capers,
methodically with old newspapers
he lined the foxholes dug below
her front porch. Nowhere else to go.

Heroin's expensive, so in time
his life became a life of crime.
Half conscious, half hysterical
he tried to rob a lounge-bar till.
Two screaming women in fur coats
got in his way. He cut their throats.

That's murder in the first degree
of course; but how he got to be
the way he was, serving his country
with what we call 'conspicuous gallantry,'
might have been thought as mitigating:

but, being preoccupied with hating
crime, we didn't think, we sent
young Funchess down for punishment
instead of help.
               Well, so it goes.
Bring back the Death-House to oppose
the tide of violence!
               Does it so?
Seventeen thousand on Death Row
are killed at a weekly rate of three,
and queues of people want to see
the killers killed, if not deterred.
Lethal injections are preferred,
but Funchess got the electric chair.

Friends of the girls he killed were there
to watch him suffer for his sins.
A snapshot shows triumphant grins.
'The grief cycle's completed there,'
concluded a philosopher;
but other souls were not so cool.
Watching him on that three legged stool
actually burning, so upset
one voyeur he could not forget.
A citizen had dreams as bad
as the dog soldier ever had.

Brief Solidarity

The thing I tripped over was a man
on the pavement. I reached out my hand
to his hand automatically.
It was dirty and hard with energy.
He refused to rise but held on. Well, that
was his business; but his old chat . . .
the usual half insulting and prolix,
pressing, non-sequiturs of alcoholics . . .
suggested no help or relationship
was possible then. So my hand slipped
his and centred on the modest hope
the immediate future would include water and soap.

The First Nervous Irrevocable Steps

It was Liam Dixon brought it in a crumpled bag.
I remember the powder, lumpy and white, inside.
He bought it off Sweeney the chemist ostensibly
for his bicycle. Ha. Ha. It was carbide.

'You can make explosions,' he told us. Action at last!
Something commensurate with grown-up fun,
the warfare we devoured in the picture houses,
sword slash, spear thrust, a burst from the Tommy Gun.

We were solemn as soldiers, conspiring and laying plans
and telling lies, to get out that winter night,
prepared and potent, indifferent to being soaked
by the dripping laurels that gleamed under streetlamp light.

We had knowledge of silent opening of gates
and aiming of bottles; one at the door to the hall,
one at the window to disturb them and bring them out.
The smell, the whitish vapour: I remember it all.

The first cork flew like a bullet, near enough.
It tapped the window. And now the carbide burned
in the second bottle . . . This cork between the eyes!
Damn! It hit the wood as the door knob turned.

A father figure in a suit was staring about
sternly, nervously, blindly, and then he was gone.
We still felt powerful, hidden, and him exposed.
The poor old fool didn't know what was going on.

Naming Your Pleasure
a spontaneous effusion for St Patrick's Day
commissioned by BBC, Belfast. 1990

1

If Patrick was haunted by Usheen's complaint
about drab apostles – he preferred hero to saint –,
ahead on the road the Scotsman, Burns, had his measure:

Get up off your knees, old man, and name your pleasure.
People like us, around our firesides, after
a hard day's work, want peace and quiet and laughter
and songs about life, where a man is his own boss.
Our eyes are fixed on our kids or our wives, I think,
or the pretty breasts of a girl, or the next drink,
or how to live better, not on you or the Cross.

2

Our National Saint, from Scotland, was a Deacon's son,
Succath, a rich and spoilt young man, Dumbarton
bred, lax in observance in early years,
his devout devoted parents often in tears
over their worldly son's weakness for flesh pots . . .
Potita, Calpurnius, Romano-Scots.

One day this pastoral, model life was split
up the middle, sadly, rudely, for into it
came a band of Irish pirates whose knives cut throats.

Succath and sisters were taken off in boats.

Warrior-farmer Milcho MacCuboin of Slemish
acquired a herder. The sisters seemed to vanish.

3

Beaten and bullied, regretting his former state,
Patrick felt guilty and was quick to hate
his deprivation. For the first time he was lonely
for Christian love, his only.

Then, 'If only . . .'
he said, seeing as blessed the old humdrum.

He felt the height that he had fallen from.

4

A deep religious feeling seems to show
through his rough Latin in 'Confessio.'

The love and fear of God was fire within
on the cold mountain, hatred of sin
that brought such punishment. Despondency
urged action, a hundred prayers a day
in snow and frost and rain before the dawn.

In him the work ethic was very strong,

rising above hardship into vision,
voices that promised him escape from prison,
and then,
        A boat is waiting on the quay.

He left his crook and his care and ran away.

5

But however far he ran he was coming back
to the land of captivity. Whatever it lacked
he had learnt to love it, the weather or the view
towards Jura, the language, or a people that never knew
Rome's law?
        Whatever it was I feel it too.

6

I was born here in Ulster, but my people came
from England and Scotland. I was Christian.
I got it at many removes from Christ's first hopes,
flirtations with secular power, the warrior popes,
the Crusades, Luther and Calvin, The Inquisition,
the decline of the Catholic Church from opposition
to the role of willing handmaid, collaborator
with any old reactionary dictator,
the scourge of every secular liberator.

The original vision of love and equity
had been handed back to the people, to poetry
and philosophy, to Rousseau and Blake. The voices
in my young day were Lawrence's and Joyce's.

The Christian word from the Derry Presbytery
was of work and obedience and sexual purity,
but the texts they quoted pushed me another way,
to be kind to women caught in adultery,
to beware of the priest and the whited sepulchre,
to cast out money-changers and love my neighbour.

I could feel Christ listening, angry, far away,
talking of love and compassion and equity,
the temptations of power and money, dispirited
that the best he could do and say had never led
to a better world. There was always some St Paul
to shift the emphasis and spoil it all.

. . . .

7

Succath reached Scotland, but Scotland was no good.
He needed the Continent to stir his blood
and intellect, to learn from serious men.
It was twenty years before he came back again.
Visions, temptations, dreams made him more and more
the perfect spiritual conquistador.
In the final dream Christ came to his command,
held out the crosier in his nail-pierced hand.
The shepherd's crook he had thrown away, restored
to the spiritual shepherd, by his Lord.

So, Patrick now, (Succath had had his day)
the perfect salesman for Christianity,
came back and persuaded violent passionate men
to accept the package of grace, to think again
about first essentials. In him power from above
released new powers in the people he'd learnt to love,
sensitive, ardent servants easily led,
but not to be driven.

8
                    Magnificent scholars they made!
They preserved their ancient legends. They illuminated
the Gospels in brilliant hues and complicated
Celtic designs and figures. The Morrigu
roosted on a capital letter and a carved pew.
From the church roof, water drained on a pious prig
from the stone sex organs of a Sheila na Gig.

In a meadow of margin of parchment holy text
a monk could note down what was happening next
outside his window in most elegant lyrics,
or a love story or the secret thoughts of clerics.
Their faith could teach the birds to sing Christ's love.
They said God bent to watch each sacred grove

smiling and listening. The little monasteries
were real enough, and the workmanship we prize
on cross and chalice and bell, the marvellous fruit,
of men who would civilise Europe;

                              but the root
must have had something rotten through and through.
We live today where all this got us to.

. . . .

9
Before the violent Danes began to ride
sea-roads and sweep the monastic world aside,
excessive spirituality came in,
the love-sense jostled by the sense of sin,
not hope so much for life as for after-life,
more solitaries than happy man and wife.

Christ really said, 'Look, we can live better.'
Now the Green party preach him to the letter,
but they'll corrupt themselves, their leading thinkers
already hound the smokers and the drinkers,
and will get round to poet, lover, joker,
forgetting Christ himself was a heavy smoker.

10
I could have gone on all St Patrick's Day,
reciting, singing to you, subtly,
of strange turns in the Irish spiritual
life and elsewhere, of who makes Heaven and Hell,
dogma, dictatorship, faith and bigotry,
pogroms and Peristroika, murder and liberty,
change and the fear of change, loving and hating;
but I grow weary of interpreting.

The high whine of the helicopter above
might be spy or conscience or descending dove.

. . . .

We need the saints, and yet we must complain.
Go back to the first stanza and start again.

The Road to Enniskillen

1

Was it Augher? Was it Clogher? Was it Fivemiletown
I was waiting in for transport as the rain came down?

We'd got a lift from Monaghan, were heading for the West.
It was sunny when we started and we both were lightly
                                                    dressed.

We arrived ahead of schedule, and the driver had to know,
in his kind heart, that we wouldn't be left standing in the
                                                    snow.

So we both of us assured him till he drove off with a frown
and gestured at the heavy clouds, but rain it was came
                                                    down

in Augher? Was it Clogher? Was it Fivemiletown?

2

I stood beside a woman I had planted in my heart.
The roots of love had settled. I could feel the growing start.

So steady and deliberate an older man can be,
to work and wait for happiness to come, deservedly.

An old man's bones are brittle and his heart is slow to heal.
At first her firm young body had seemed lovely but unreal.

She waited at the corner while I bought a bag of chips
to finger from the paper and lift steaming to our lips.

3

The glossy limousine drew up, a cargo of good craic.
A quirky little poetess was giggling in the back,

and to calm her palpitations I must gently squeeze her hand
in keeping with traditions of the poets of that land.

Uneasy, we were driven down the road towards Enniskillen
to pay a tribute to the dead with speeches by the living.

The gabble gradually stilled. Thoughts of the dead can drown
all jealousy and vanity and need to act the clown.

Was it Augher? Was it Clogher? Was it Fivemiletown?

4

'If you go to Enniskillen,' she could hear her lover say,
'you're a traitor, to salute the dead and blame the IRA.

There are many dead, some fresh and more from older wars
                                        than these,
that suffered cruelly from the crimes of Ireland's enemies.

You're going out of vanity. I know you well,' said he.
'If you go to Enniskillen, you need not come back to me.'

But she went although she loved him and was scared of him.
                                        She knew,
for Ireland, there are some things that a person must not do.

So she giggled out of nervousness and watched the rain come
                                        down
over Augher, over Clogher, over Fivemiletown.

Our Castles are Ruins or Hotels
a free version after the Irish of Nuala Ní Dhomhnaill

In your arms, lover, whoever you are,
I know I will never die,
safe there from sudden panic
or terror that takes over.
I will never jerk awake
and say, 'Sorry, sorry,'
scared in the quiet night
by brakes screeching, or not the river
whispering under our window,
but the engine of a big lorry.

Your arms are a safe house
in the countryside, your shoulders
the outhouses and yard
where not even a mouse
stirs. The world that threatens
is beyond the farthest meadows.
I have been looking for a long lease,
safety from the bad luck
of my people, ascendancy
at last, a walled garden
where lovers can fuck in peace.

The English made such gardens,
kingdoms for honey-bees
that moved from flower to flower
under the apple trees.
They were harsh, efficient soldiers
and gardeners, builders of walls
behind which everything grows
far into Autumn, comfortable
when the North wind blows.

We can watch on television,
empire building, nations and races
at war . . . hurt and destruction
over the face of the earth,
and turn it off and turn to each other.
If all the four zones of the globe
go up in one sad explosion,
if the cosmos coagulates
in one dire fusion,

why should I care? Your arms
caressing my bare skin,
what would I know of fear or anger,
of mad dogs devouring each other
out there, or even pity?
All my urges are gratified
when you gather me up gently,
a woman, a light parcel,
safe and well, freeholder
in the sensual city.

For always keep me close
to your powerful glow,
the magic circle of body heat,
skin against skin and the flesh below,
your mouth dipping towards me,
my hair, my thighs, my breasts.
How could I know or care
for wolves howling
in some distant street?

Do you not think I know
that sooner or later the sweetest lover
will give me a distancing kiss
on the forehead and let me go
in solitude to my own side,
turning like a cold fish, exiled,
in what feels like an empty bed?

Did I think he might wait a while?

Could I think that in truer arms,
I might never have died?

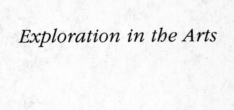

Exploration in the Arts

For Philip Larkin

Your verse is elegantly seedy,
taking away and sliding back.
You punctured our inflated hopes
in sonorous Tennysonian tropes,
offering integrity for lack
of hope, superior to the needy

(ciphers for you, or petty hates),
the sentimental groom and bride,
all those who buy the shoddy ware
in shopping centres, while you stare,
a cold observer at their side
who can't imagine their estates,

cramped settings of their griefs and flings.
You watched one 'larking with the mails,'
stupid, you seemed to think, and dull,
pathetic, something one might mull
over and pin down with nails
of verse. You were one who noticed such things.

I loved you, but it must be said,
though you spoke of a cure, you were never free
of Romance. There were more tricks than flesh
in your rhetoric . . . 'Afresh, afresh!'
You weren't safe near an estuary,
and twice in church you lost your head.

The North Ship never was alive?
Art gulled you like the Church gulled Joyce.
It must be almost like being ill
at that age to be gullible
to that extent, assume a voice
so totally derivative.

Your true persona seems to me
plain but not gauche, with cycle clips.
The no-hope-hero cuts up rough,
freeing us of all romantic guff,
a literary Sir Stafford Cripps,
connoisseur of austerity.

Ageing delinquent, kicking Arts
in the balls, leaving the urge to live
to mugs, you relished what you hated.
Joy and panache, unique, belated,
came in *High Windows*, negative,
beautifully timed and crafted farts.

Oh, there was jazz and melancholy
landscapes you loved, clearly the thrill
of writing sharply, facing the void
with all the coolness of an android.
Bored, always bored, then old and ill,
with no illusions, nothing holy.

I see I'm one of those you hated,
who could see no alternative
to getting down to love and work
when we could get it. Jill meets jerk:
we talk, we fuck, we fight, we live.
We kid ourselves and get deflated

and wake up with our chills and bruises,
and then repeat the same mistakes.
Like the rude jazz of Charlie Mingus
dark, lonely work, like cunnilingus,
is what the needy undertakes
and relishes before he loses.

You made a pact to tell no lies,
Faustus of that bleak generation,
and played at being terrified
of life, and died before you died,
a poet without inspiration,
the object of the exercise.

An Ulster Prospero

for John Hewitt

A jutting bearded profile
ready for a fight,
puritan, pontifical
and usually right.

Captain McWhirr of Ulster,
as you flowered, as you aged,
half competent, half impotent,
while the typhoon raged.

What foul play was it
sent you to Coventry?
Or was it a hidden blessing,
to let you get away?

A Protestant Prospero
who, of course, abjured
magic of any sort,
leaves the island uncured,

old dogs still in office.
Although your gifts were ample
what can we say you left us,
John, a map, an example,

your work alive and kicking
in our heads, in our hearts.
After a life of service
your body is spare parts.

Cavalier and Roundhead

i.m. John Hewitt

I was away when you died, John.
I was always away. That house
in Stockman's Lane
where once you welcomed me
I never visited again.

Ageing on my young wife's bosom
I would say, 'We must see John!'
Restive, incredulous,
she'd murmur, 'Count me out,'
and I betrayed you. I betrayed us.

At tepid literary gatherings
when we walked towards each other
there was something in the air,
a warm salute, then silence
that we seemed to share.

I know you used dour silence
to cause discomfiture,
for you were dour, and sly,
testing. But not to be questioned
suited me. We were both shy.

Then I was looking for a pint,
or distracted by pretty breasts,
when it was your place
I should have gone to and learned
to read that unattractive face.

Talent's not everything.
I need knowledge and discipline
to become one of the elect,
to wrestle an angel of your stature,
even to reject.

73

Coming from different ends
of the Protestant spectrum,
I was your rightful heir
I thought, but you were suspicious.
Of what? Of my curly hair?

Were you hurt I never turned up
for the sound advice, the lore?
I was getting stewed or kissed,
my old foolish addictions.
I'll never know what I missed.

So, when the honours fell like manna,
and you, crustily, allowed
the Lord Mayor to seduce
you and The Workers' Party,
I was of no use.

You trembled at the microphone,
complaining of lost standards,
accepting Seamus and Jack
and Davy, with this freedom and that
medal, instead of saying, 'I lack

nothing without you, and hand on
to my not so young friend
the stewardship against lies,
that I have lived for
and he exemplifies.'

But my last mention on your lips
was to ask a mutual friend,
forlorn, but smiling grimly,
'What is that scallywag up to?'
You loved, you needed, me.

The Savoy Sessions
'keeping company'
(An account of some recordings made by John Birks
Gillespie and friends in Detroit 1951)

1
The first famous recordings of Bop were intense
and austere revelations. These are indulgence,
unbuttoned minutes with the ascended star
maybe day-dreaming of being popular.
I find a virtue in unevenness.
The labour that let these sessions come to pass
was a sort of cottage industry, perhaps,
a fan supporting the giant when contracts lapsed
with the big labels – fame's embrace and recoil.
The benefactor's father was in oil.

Bar talk: 'The big boys left you in the lurch.
I love your music. I hate market research.
We'll lay down just what grabs us, you and me.
My sis does graphics. I'm calling it *Dee Gee*,
out of your own initials, ain't that cute?'
He ran the flag up, watching Diz salute.

They shook hands and it happened. It was Dave
Usher was the angel's name, a man to rave
at the back of the hall, pay the rent and the needy
out of his hip pocket. Hip indeedy!

The central group was Jackson, Heath, Burrell;
but the youngster, John Coltrane, is there as well,
part of the late big band. And the first Bop
trombonist, J.J. Johnson, just turned up.
Bud Johnson and Stuff Smith, for me,
were the cream, old masters in young company.

The revolution had required a coterie,
but any damned musician who could play
pleased Diz. So here's Detroit in '51,
four sessions, some good jazzmen having fun.

2
There were a few Bop classics to revamp:
Tin Tin Deo, Birks Works, The Champ.
Then a few standards, *Stardust* and *Caravan*;
but why record *Schooldays, Umbrella Man*,
old vaudevilles? A joke? Or an insult
to those who hailed the priest of a new cult?
In *Pops Confessin* Diz parodies the master.
His loving accuracy brought down the house,
like Larkin doing Hardy or Gershwin, Strauss.
Only the final bunch are a disaster,
novelty songs in the current Bop argot
that once seemed smart, now a corpse in the cargo.
Dizzie hired singers, three of them, third rate
Billy Ecksteins, unmusical, up to date.
Why did he do it? What else can be said,
but they were crudely aimed at The Hit Parade.

A strong producer might have carried the thing . . .
but shit, who cares? I'd rather hear Stuff swing
implacably through *Sunny Side of the Street*
and endure the vocals than listen to effete
stylistically perfect, groomed occasions
with all the oddballs out, and orchestrations!

Six years before this Monk and Parker and Diz
had invented Bop. You know what the story is,
the innovation script, where no one listens
or they laugh. Even the experts, good musicians
are sure it is ugly music. You feel it so,
then it gets under our skins so much that Jo
Stafford is making with comical Bop breaks

in her pop routines. So innovation takes
and becomes the feel of the present, 'modern jazz.'
The apparent gimmick has what all art has.

3
The rebels can board a bandwagon that creaks
with hip jargon and scholarly critiques.
The spreads in *Time* and *Life* were a glossy waste,
condescending, with errors of fact and taste;
but Hampton's explications were the best of craic:
'Bepop is really the chord structure, Mack.
Rebop's the rhythm; but Zoobop and Oobop are BIG
concepts, beyond definition. Dig?'

Bird and Diz, radically different,
appeared like twins in a world they were intent
on outfacing. The handsome visage was closed down
when Bird was playing. Diz chose to act the clown
with black beret, blowing a bent horn,
and he's still blowing. Parker is long gone.
Bird was volcanic genius, ignited flow,
Gillespie, a scholar virtuoso,
both unapologetically black,
apparently unaware of this as a set-back.
Parker treated the audience like shit.
Diz could satyrically make love to it,
beret and goatee from Bohemia? France?
The bent horn seemed to promise falling pants.
His smile was absolutely superior,
and the difficult phrasing and high notes he went for.

4
Bud Johnson and Stuff Smith! How they seem
to draw the innovators into the main stream.
Diz is relaxed and majestic, one of the boys,
extremely talented boys. You know he enjoys
the gruffly subtle, thrusting obbligato
of the old jazz fiddler urging him, 'Go, man. Go.'

In *Stardust* Stuff insists on a few sustained
elemental notes. The trumpeter is unchained.
He might be Armstrong, Eldridge, King Oliver
or Clayton or George Mitchell. You can't tell where
the style is coming from, early or late;
but you know he belongs with music. He's one of the great.

It was only three years later that Norman Granz
galvanised Dizzie again with his carte blanche,
Jazz at the Philharmonic;
                but hear again:
the first recorded solo of John Coltrane,
Milt Jackson's vibes, 'like juggling with stars,'
Johnson announcing his presence in a few bars,
in *Birks Works* the blithe and pointed quote
that discovers a blues phrase in *The Volga Boat.*
The pyrotechnics are strong and bendy as wire
in *The Champ*, and he turns the band into a choir
for *Swing Low, Sweet Cadillac*, with a sigh
in the last cadence . . . 'Cadillacs never die . . .'

It was good to get rid of the brilliant broken-backed
phrasing that made Bop, Bop, to let flair and tact
and diverse talents flower in pleasant ways.

Dizzie still gets requests to play *Schooldays*
and is glad to oblige, smiling, remembering
that lull in the revolution, that private spring.

'Dammit, we never did make any money,
but I still wish we could have kept the company.'

The Egotist's Teddy Wilson

From LP covers I know all I know:
two years before my birth, in Chicago
Teddy was playing with Louis professional piano.

But my actual birth year was the real starter:
he hit New York along with Benny Carter
soul-mates playing never defter nor smarter.

When I was being educated, caned on the hand,
Teddy got almost famous with the Goodman band.
(Too damn noisy for my taste, boomy and bland.)

Between the popular concerts he was at his best,
recording with Billie, Buck Clayton and Lester
in pick-up sessions. They tell me he invoked Alastor,

spirit of solitude, that he stuck to his stride
style, strict if subtle. Let Lester glide
over the beat and hover, let Billie slide

behind and across his structured frames of light
emphatic notes. 'Teddy, you're uptight,'
they told him, smiling. We all knew he was right.

I heard him first in the fifties, by perfect chance,
and listened enough to let his art enhance
my sketchy life with true cool elegance.

The Wallace Collection

It was Launchbury in his villa at Twickenham
suggested a visit to The Wallace, and here I am.

God, but London's exhausting. One tires less
on weekends hiking in the wilderness.

What stairs and concrete alleys in search of a pee
at Marble Arch! Give me the moors and scree.

I labour with suitcase and parcels, LPs and books
through this metropolis of tarts and crooks.

I was banned from the National Gallery, laden thus;
but The Wallace accommodates baggage without fuss.

Attendants, attentive but slightly plump in the arse,
suggest femininity, for better or worse.

Why do I think they are queer, on a fleeting visit?
For unusual softness, a lack of frankness, is it?

Natures that can't declare themselves? Ah no.
That way's been cleared by many a martyr hero.

Much too much for the mind to grapple. I shirk
philosophy and wander round the work.

Richard Parkes Bonington . . . a marvellous start!
Landscapes and rain and sunshine taken to his heart.

Abroad and brave and talented, with a marvellous eye,
technique and draughtsmanship . . . and about to die.

How well he filled his life and filled the page
achieve all this and die at half my age!

Survivor Rembrandt was drawn to warts and all,
dignity living with awkward detail.

Greuze, the old pornographer of Paris,
is the ideal illustrator for Frank Harris.

His *Child with Lamb* will surely perform on request.
Look at those moistened lips, that peeping breast.

What excitements of red and white in Rubens. You could view
them
as abstract colour masses, but there's more to them.

Such masters offer us many tensions. He controls
a riot of colour and examines bodies and souls.

The white on the nose and the chain, the red hat
on his son, are only a part of what Rembrandt's at.

Colours on living objects are an extra theme.
Pollock's just lines and texture and colour scheme.

The guide at The Tate said, 'Surely one thinks of dancers
on a prairie.' Surely not. Experts are chancers.

I love these small collections that only show
a handful of masterpieces you can get to know.

Back to the counter for postcards as the mind soaks
images up and ideas and brush strokes.

My bags seem lighter. I leave with smiling face
to dine with the Foleys in a little Italian place.

Intruder on Station Island
(supposed to be spoken by Seamus Heaney)

I expected the next ghost to shake hands
would equal in fame my previous advisers.
Yeats? Swift? No, they were Protestants.

Imagine my chagrin to feel leather on bone,
a boot up my arse from a former rugby player,
shade of a Catholic policeman I had known.

'Seamus, oul' son, how are ye? I was reading your book in
Mullan's. Where's all the imitations and jokes
you regaled us with? They don't get a look in.

And weemin? Ye must have had many a wee frolic
with hot things in Harvard and the West Coast,
but never a mention, or if there is it's symbolic!'

I expounded my aunt's old leather trowel,
its handle an egret's head, a furled sail,
the rounded hanging lip an Irish vowel;

but he interrupted and had the impudence
to advise me: 'Relax, oul' hand. Enjoy your luck,
but give us a rest from the weather and farm implements.'

From a cattle-dealing line that would stretch from the Boyne
to Lough Neagh, crookedly, a prefect of *St Columb's*,
I knew how to knee a nuisance in the groin;

but signed pamphlets are more effective than dunts.
I keep them about me. This one argued fiercely
that Faber should pay its Irish poets in punts.

How to escape without giving offence was my pain!
To aid me the air stirred my blow-dried hair
as a helicopter whose pilot was Craig Raine

descended. The nonentity melted in whipped air.

Comic Relief
for George Formby Snr

The comedian had poor health
most of his forty years. Wealth
flowed in painfully. Being ill
was the joke, the cough was bronchial.
'I am coffin tonight' was his catch-line,
pulling a long face. They liked it fine.

'I know how money should be spent,'
he said to the suave estate agent,
pulling a wad from his pocket.
'If I'm not here to enjoy it
the family will. Comic relief!'
He spat blood in his handkerchief.

The Happy Worrier

'Professor Jeffares,' I said, but you were merry:
'Drop the bloody handle. Call me Derry.'
I sat beside you listening to the same
lecture, inwardly giggling at that name,
my eyes fixed on your neat trousers, aware
that underneath would be blanched skin and hair,
that you were a forked animal like me.
That seemed to be true only in theory
for your power made me tremble, and I choked
with nerves and a sort of anger the more you joked.
They were Professors' jokes. And so the stance
I took up waveringly was defiance
though even at the time I was ashamed,
even in self-defence, to be unkind.
You didn't notice or you didn't mind.
Presuming you didn't have to justify
good will by knowing my quality was a lie.
I wasn't content to be in the category,
'bright student, acceptable.' I was ME.

And nothing has changed. I am a grey-haired
lecturer now; but my students don't seem scared
of the power I have to judge them. They feel free.
I'd rather be scared of them than them of me.
They make or waste themselves. On *their* whim,
not at my invitation, they call me, 'Jim.'

I was the virtuous one in my own eyes
in that poem years ago. I apologise.
I was just lucky with my students, now I can see,
luckier, Derry, than you were with me –
in too much of a hurry to be at the top.
To promote myself I measured you for the drop

and listened to gossip that made you shallow and bland,
less interested in poems than in command,
who must have felt some qualms, uncertainty,
filling the chair of Bonamy Dobree.
But, leaning on Wordsworth, the final verse still stands,
a bright ideal shaped with dirty hands:

I am looking for teachers who need less bluff than nerve,
who don't solicit more than they deserve
of deference, who cultivate a sense
and faculty for storm and turbulence,
who won't stir trouble up, but will endure
and expect it, sustaining grace under pressure,
style and a sense of form under duress,
although their master-bias leans to quietness.

Boats in a Tempest

The big wave followed us down.
I was the helmsman, damp arse
wedged on the bench, aching ribs
of my right side jammed to starboard,
sole of my left foot pressed
hard down for purchase. Facing
desperately ahead I could feel
walls of water feeling me up,
dribbling on neck and shoulders.

It didn't feel like sailing,
sliding down the trough, lost
to the wind. There was no weight
for man and rudder to lean against
steering. Still, a wave runs
by laws, powerful but not surprising.
There was no malice in this grabbing
and buffeting. I could concentrate

undistracted by detail, smiling,
I seem to remember, noticing
foam in odd places, like cherry
blossom over our heads and elegant
whirls and eddies, and another boat,
glimpsed, rising gratefully
out of a neighbour trough, having taken
the same path downward.

None of us drowned.

The Integrity of Jo Kidd

Discharged after a calculated night
in gaol after an evening's drinking
they brought him in from prison chores
unshaven and moving at his own speed,

                                                    slowly.

Here was one who travelled light.

You wouldn't say that he was thinking,
owning nothing but his durable clothes,
well worn.
                    We saw his calm as something holy.

His boots were stylish and well made
and fairly ornate.
                    Then, as of right,
he claimed back the revolver he explored
expertly, looking down the sight,

then buckled on his gun belt, nothing said,
doused his head under the pump.

                                        Complete,
and everybody waiting, he faced the hard
well-armed bunch of strangers in the prison yard.

They were hunting Chama, a Mexican Robin Hood.
They offered this thing of dust
five hundred dollars – he was that good –
to guide them in this territory, his
by knowledge.
                    'No,'
                                He shook his head and just

turned away from their anger.

                            Our hearts were full,
greedy and frightened, chastened at no excuse,
no mind searching, no fear . . .
                            it was beautiful.

Here was a model of integrity, created
by writer, actor and director,
                            but it fell apart
when the action got more complicated.

The film had plenty of style but no heart.

Chama,
        that Jo had refused to hunt,
                            did Jo
a bad turn, and Jo followed the outlaws
on his own.
            He was ingenious at killing off
opponents.
            Chama wasn't so smart as Kidd,
he got tired and frightened and even developed a cough.

He would never outwit the law like Jo did
who had no ideas or affections to give him pause.

For Chama it was prison or death. I was quite upset
by the moral vacuum.

                    The times seemed out of joint

if Jo could ride with the girl into the sunset

smiling at a joke.

                Unless that was the point.

Former Relationships

Addiction

The manic urge dies
after any real bliss,
but not a love like this
that never satisfies.

The Sex Object Doesn't Object

Raised up above me by his arms
he looks down to make a study
of what we both see as my charms.

Therefore I feel my cunt fizz.
I want him to enjoy my body
as I enjoy his.

Years After

You were rank as an old harbour
with hidden decaying fish.
To rub my nose in your corners
was my one constant wish.

All your curves were shining,
your belly and your breasts.
Your hair was a dark forest,
your armpits little nests.

Wandering up to the kitchen
the moonlit walls were wet.
Smoking and sipping coffee
we lounged in our sweat,

your head against my shoulder,
my mouth against your brow,
more gentle and more tender
than ever we are now.

The Positive Cynic

Hunger to live in love
taught us to lie,
you to admire Bing Crosby,
me to imply
I'd always put down books
if you were by.

But don't think badly of us,
wife, tonight.
Good sexual intercourse
is such delight
that any means to get your end
seems right.

Caught in our kindly lies,
wanting release,
you wince when I play guests
my old LPs
I smile when you're too tired,
and read in peace.

If you had been more scrupulous
in stating
your tastes, and said
mine were excruciating . . .
if we'd waited for soul mates
we'd still be waiting.

Loneliness

It alerts the emotions
like a flourish of trombones
announcing romantic arrival,
the whisper of car tyres on gravel,
powdery earth and tiny stones
smoothed out level,
the landing strip before the threshold.

The noise is incalculable
though I feel it in my bones.

No, the visitor is next door.
I am stood up, a smiling clown
welcoming interruption once more.

Sit down. Sit down!

A Message to the Wife

That little kiss this evening
as the cocktails went round
was love, my lady. Your decency
your straight talk are lovely,
but the quick endorsement of lips
is the truest, the only. It makes sense.
Who lack faith live by evidence,
and you aren't romantic, you don't say,
'I love you,' easily.

My case rests on this. Last night
you had lost me, remember. I seem
to live detached till the welding happens
again and now again. Our nakedness
was not drowsy. The mystery stripped us
farther, beyond affection, Emmanuelle,
touchy, brutal, exploitive,
wanting and taking all that we were.
Dirty and full of nerve, a perfect fit,
demand was supplied. Raw material met
means of production, didn't it?

To suit me just right, darling,
I shifted your body about.
To be laid and lifted suited you
into the small hours of the night.
Lips moist and melting, every
spontaneous touch a small explosion,
as hands, inspired and sweaty, were shaping
backbone, breasts and thighs. The piston
drive of prick and cunt blossomed in sighs.
Delicate, delectable, trembling and sore
and thirsty, you cried out marvellous lies

when we could take no more. 'The only
honest bone in my body is yours.'
Such sacramental small obscenities.

Tonight the brief conventional
salute of lips, as the cocktails
went round, commemorated
a battle of the great war. We are
veterans, proudly bruised and scarred.

When the Women Have Gone to Bed

Your hand reaches me down, the square bottle
of Jim Beam from your sister's drinks
cupboard. The glasses are on the shelf
above, tumblers, too big for whisky.
Choose the smallest and pour a measure
with your eye, the way you learnt
in the bar trade. The years have made you
generous so the customers are lucky,
and you are the customer.

Me? I'm a slightly overflavoured
whisky, perfumed and rough, sour mash.
Under the tap take care. Let it run
steady before you proffer the glass.
It never works to undilute
from the bottle. Whisky's a short
never a thirst quencher, and drinking
from brimming tumblers misses
the point. It's tasteless and dangerous.

Set your glass down and put me away.
This is the last drink tonight.
Dowse the kitchen lights and carry
your glass back to that easy chair
whose square arm seems to be made for
ashtray and glass. Fag lit, lift
Tanner's *The Reign of Wonder*, the chapter
on Hemingway. Sip, take a drag.

Remember this. You misunderstand me
if you think you need more, if you think
of the next glass before you start
on this one. Drink me, be happy, read
till your mind wanders, then go to bed.
If you reach for another, I warn you
I'll be different tomorrow
and emptier than you expected.

Friday Morning
(the poet again falls in love with his wife)

In Belfast all late drinkers know
the Paramour's the place to go.
On the window sill of room fourteen,
happy this morning as I've ever been
with a book and a cigarette and tea
I read with nothing bugging me.
Over the streets and houses streams
new sunlight. This is within my means
and that's the pleasure, to read in peace
in a very private unprivileged place.

Stuck for a kip last night we came
to this seedy bedroom, this gilt frame
round a garish landscape, 'ancient mill
by murky river' after Constable.
The colour scheme of walls and bed
is Eau de Nile on Wino Red.
'The ashtray,' my dear love opined,
'is the one object well designed,'
undressing to her flame silk slip.
What heights of good companionship.

She's gone, but evidences stay:
our crippled butts in that ashtray,
our soiled glasses, the faint sting
of her perfume. What I was just now reading
was a few poems by Kathleen Raine.
I expected a neo-Platonic pain
in the arse; but no, no! I was wrong.
Plain and intense she achieves song.
Oh, not too often, she is abstract;
but you can catch her in the act.

'Pity and tenderness in the marriage bed,'
she prays for.

Embracing couples are often dead
to the world; but lithe-frame rode sweet shiny-ass
last night!

Let cleaners come for the soiled glass
and ashtray. Let fresh linen and laundered towels
be brought for tonight's lovers and night owls.
May they rise as tender, as early, as my wife and I,
and descend to shiny teapot and Ulster fry.

A Woman's Company
(a song)

I need a woman's company,
a place to rest my head,
few words, a woman's company
to share my board and bed.
Soft arms, some gentle flattery,
laughter when I amuse,
wise-cracks if I'm obstreperous,
a modest taste for booze.

I need a woman's company,
but I must watch my ways.
Lovers seem too miraculous
in those first heady days.
Lies told will lead to misery,
false smiles become a smirk.
Nice girls shine out in galaxies,
but courtship is hard work.

Living is mostly loneliness,
our empty arms reach out.
Our mouths will babble anything . . .
that's what love's all about:
'Hold me, my darling. Love me, my darling.
Kiss me and part your thighs.
Take me, my darling, praise me, my darling.'
Both partners drown in sighs.

Pure sex? Impossibility!
Well maybe once or twice.
Those soft desirous entities
can turn out not so nice.
Nervousness curbs ability,
greed coarsens every touch.
She longed to share eternity,
but now a month's too much.

Do I need a woman's company?

The Return

An old tipsy ass astray on the rocks,
he came back to the scene of his marriage nervous of
shocks;
but since he was in the town and between two trains
he wanted, he told himself, a word with the weans.

There wasn't a light in the place. Were they all away?
He opened the door and felt a way in quietly
and came on a tableau vivant to haunt his mind:
the person he once knew best in the world entwined
in a centaur's embrace, laughing, shrieking, blowing
heavily, kicking the creature off but allowing
liberties, joylessly. It leered and bound
across the room to take her, and was shaken down
like a wave off rocks, wrestler's arms trailing
over her breasts, the woman laughing and railing.
The sounds she uttered were strange to his twenty years
as husband to that wife. His startled ears
contrasted these with the sounds he had inspired.
She was new for the new man!
                                Do they respond as required,
women?

            It seemed what he watched was passing slowly,
like a vision, this keyhole moment, ugly, unholy
and wholly fascinating. He couldn't bring
himself to remove. Their eyes met, recognising
nothing. It wasn't erotic or pornographic.
She might have been playing with a dog; but the thick
brute was human, a bruiser, a fat boy,
fantastic exercise, an unspeakable toy.

Didn't Chekov suggest they remake themselves to fit?
The darlings, the bitches! 'The men demanded it.'
But inventing a self for this one! He could think she might
have done it to demean herself. She was sick with spite.
Or she might have discovered her real self at last.
Whatever it was he pushed the door close fast,
quietly, longing to question, walking away,
divorced from the right to question intimately.

Eating Hens' Feet

1

Taken out for a treat
to 'the restaurant most respected
by Toronto's Chinese,'
we were threatened by good taste.
Those weren't bright rissoles
but legs of hens to eat.
I gagged, gag still, remembering
those ominously glittering,
cast in gold, hens' feet.

So much sophisticated stuff
I don't relish, though I might try,
out of an urge to celebrate
maybe. 'Let's go out to the All My Eye
for a real splurge!'; but the guff
and the waiting to order, and the hate
you conceive for the pompous waiter,
and the prices that are really beyond us.
Almost all of it would taste better
at home. I am forced. I hate the fuss!

Today at The Café Montmartre
sausage and egg and chips was so perfectly
what I wanted, for a start,
followed by bread and tea.
There is such freshness in the ordinary,
and you hardly bother your head
choosing, you eat and read.

2

Too much ambition can confuse your needs.
The happiest moment, maybe, in my life
was in a transport café outside Leeds,
sausage and eggs and chips, with my first wife,

about to enter the city, the promised land,
get any job to see the summer past,
a seedy flat, a book case, second-hand.
When September came I would be a student at last.

I wiped the savoury grease with a piece of bread
and opened my paperback, Turgenev's 'Hunter's Sketches.'
To hell with quails in Frascati's. I bent my head,
engrossed by the prose, at home with fellow wretches.

Rubbing the steamed up window for a look
at rain on lorries, I lit our fags, leaned back.
My sweetheart, too, was busy at her book.
She'd face the tempest in her Pacamac.

African Poems

No Ties

A sequence of love poems.
Written in the early 70's.
Published as a pamphlet by
The Honest Ulsterman Press,
excerpts from which appeared
in various later collections.
This is a complete and revised
version with an additional poem.

*'Emer, said Cuchulain, it may be true that I have
broken my vow to you; but where is the gravity of the fault?
How could I not love Fand too? She is fairer than the fair,
more beautiful than the beautiful; intelligent and talented
and a fit wife for any king and moreover has a mind that is as
keen and able as the best. There is nothing under heaven that
a wife would do for her dear husband that Fand has not done
for me. Therefore do not lay too much blame on us. And as
for yourself, where else would you find anyone who has loved
you as I have or who shows you so much
reflected honour?'*
The Sickbed of Cuchulain
trans, Eoin Neeson.

The Fortunate Fall
for Gill Gordon

They thought I owed you promises. I knew
that such insurance would embarrass you.
It didn't take much courage to defy
these nuts. I didn't need to justify
myself or you or what we feel.
They are fantastic creatures, we are real.

The V.C. at the interview talked crap
solemnly, said the threatened rap
was *moral turpitude* . . . !
I thought I might take pleasure in being rude,
inquiring just what ethical authority
running this shambles of a university
gave him? But in the end I had a try
explaining. Then we shook hands and said goodbye
across his man-in-power's crammed table.

It was all painless, even enjoyable:
I was to understand he understood,
but . . . Caesar's wife . . . the public mind is crude.
That's teaching, Gill. There always is some jerk
like him to get round to get at your work.

Now we'd be laughing, if only we could leave
together, free in exile, Adam and Eve.

The First Morning

The morning after, I drove you into work
glowing beside me in the semi dark.
The dusty sun rose up behind your head.
We seemed to be driving along the sea bed.
The night sky was the looming underside
of a grey freighter drifting on the tide.
We zoomed along towards Zaria, playing at hurry.
In our position how could we worry?

During our progress up Governor's Road
brightness began to glow
on mealy barked Fatache trees, shadowed
by warm thumb smudges of brown.
The Harmattan was bringing crisp leaves down.
Autumn, I thought.
There is no Autumn in this latitude –
the leaves just fall off,
dry trees drown in sunlight.

The car stopped in the holy stillness
of that parking lot where you departed,
appearing at the driver's window for a kiss
and disappearing without a word, getting on
with your life. My white Taunus and I were consecrated
in your service, sitting immobile when you had gone.

Tired by the happy vigil of last night
I recline in my garden with coffee. Birds sing.

My only duty is to pick you up this evening.

Revelation

My love has thick ankles
her hips are too fat.
I never expected
I'd put up with that.

In theory I knew,
but in practice demurred,
there is often more fun
with the dowdier bird.

Out here in the tropics
we're easier pleased
since whores got expensive
and brusque and diseased.

My bachelor's Taunus,
grey leather and chrome,
drives up for young women
I'd call plain at home.

Today, wide shorts flapping
and shirt out of style,
my jokes make this heavy
young graduate smile.

We read or just sit
when there's nothing to say,
and we don't have to lean
on each other all day.

She looks up in welcome.
I look down and trace
intelligence, humour
and warmth in her face,

where once I could only
see fuzzy, dry hair,
a weak chin, a poor skin,
a short-sighted stare.

Convenience became
revelation today.
'You are lovely. I love you,'
I heard myself say.

Nice Girl's Thoughts

The facts are weak beside the things that seem
as, over me, you wrestle with your dream.

Watching responses, measuring my sighs,
you ask me, straight out, when it's over,
eager for praise but quickly on to lies.

I love you, not your prowess as a lover.

I like to breathe beside you in the night.
Frank Harris couldn't lure my kind away.

An inch or so from heaven? No! The flight
is astronomical.
                    We travel it each day.

Diary Notes

1

Like Brussels Sprouts on their stalk
I fancy your little breasts as you walk
to the wash basin stripped to the waist.
Like Brussels sprouts, an acquired taste.

2

'My bonny breasts are small but they're growing,'
you sing about the house, well knowing
that constant use is how to make them grow.
They'll be worth showing off before I go.

3

I love your skipping style on the dance floor.
It is you exactly and therefore
beautiful, being true. Is there not
enough of me in my Slow Foxtrot?
If you are bad art I am a joke;
but when I bounce with you I boke.

4

The Adulteress giggled. Wind tickled her hair
through which sun blazed. Her chin was rough and red
with kissing. He had misgivings. 'I don't care.
I don't care. I am very happy,' she said.

5

Me dressed, the cook not overwrought,
five minutes late, my gravel and your car
make the noise *happiness*. I thought
you might not come, but here you are.

Dangerous Liaisons

When my wife took the children home for a while
I fell in love with a girl and felt the pain
like strenuous exercise. Gesture and style
I thought had stiffened in me came again.

What luckless people label *dirty weekends*
we lived for, inconvenienced but undaunted.
It seems that lovers can be friends.
It's a good feeling, knowing what you've always wanted.

We had both been so unlucky in the past,
both used to disappointment, that the way
happiness was happy and able to last
for weeks, for months, wasn't ordinary.

All clouds and sunrise when we separated,
cocky with love rather than broken-hearted,
I flew home to the wife I no longer hated
to share my wisdom. Then the trouble started.

'I'm flying home,' I thought, 'well-used, augmented,
back to your arms, my children and the rest.
The engine roars although the body's dented.
My sweet, your own old crock has passed the test!'

But my eyes shifted from her hungry eyes,
kissing was sacrilege, asleep in bed
my arms reached for a woman twice her size.
Poor wife, I nearly drove her off her head.

And after that we were never right again.
I thought we might live better than before,
but the humiliation, the shock of pain,
had broken something good deeds can't restore.

The End of the Affair

We could count the times we went for a walk
or the times we danced together these few months past,
if not the times of making love and talk.
Our first separation will be our last.

I suppose we hardly discussed what we have known,
that I am to go home, that you will stay.
All of the mutual tenderness that has grown,
sweet as it is, is not to get in the way

of the work before us, mine and yours.
What has been given is being taken away,
and we aren't looking for loopholes or cures,
freely absenting ourselves from felicity

to tell our story under plain covers
in bed, by example, till everyone understands
that joy will not be bound. Artists and lovers
start and complete their work with empty hands.

To leave my wife and children for love's sake
and marry you would be a failure of nerve.
I remember love, and all that goes to make
the marriage, the affairs, that I deserve.

Bigger Than Both of Us

Dry season nearly over, air loaded
with wild electric. Near twilight
we wandered into the bush. The sky exploded
with rain, making purple night.
We staggered back to the rest-house
to be enclosed by filthy brown
bedroom walls, lying down
for the last time, you quiet as a mouse.

Asleep? Flick . . . your eyes open again,
staring, dumb, unable to resist
my patter as the healing hypnotist,
grateful for thunder, the wall-rattler, rain
unloading on the roof.

                           We devoured each other
once. Sweat was our element. Discoveries
were sweet. Now what I'm feeling might appease
a child. Harmless and useless as a brother.

This way adulteries end . . . a famished kiss
before we dress at the half hour
and separate. We have time but no desire.

You talked strong, but I thought you'd come to this,
trembling and starting like a frightened horse.

I stroke your head. The great storm runs its course.

I'll Never Say Goodbye

At the end of the Serpentine,
Lancaster Gate,
on a morning last January
having to wait,
I walked where we used to walk,
fifteen years gone,
by the elegant, worn away
fountains of stone.

Like a stone-shattered windscreen
the water rose bright
against air on the left
and black trees on the right.
With small swans beside them,
in stone, at their ease,
were two big girls holding
their ewers on their knees.

Exactly your features,
the strength of your back,
the curve of your breasts
and the chin that you lack.
Your body a fountain
with life thrusting out,
and this must be the sister
you told me about.

This is my part of London,
I'm happy to know
that your statue looks down
where I once used to row,
and whenever I pass here
on poetry tours,
by the Serpentine fountains
my time will be yours.

The Heart of Brightness

Such heat the whole year round is kind to life.
Cheap servants make things easier for my wife,
but not my servants' wives. New plants grow bright
ample and vulnerable in weeks. By day and night
I could walk out in sandals, but snakes thrive
and scorpions. All living things are so alive
they choke each other. Growth is so unwilling
to be curbed it breeds intensity of killing.
Lust burgeons in this climate. So does hate.
We find it is more urgent to discriminate,
and harder, for this sun, this soft air blurs
vision – the energy cold winds of Antrim stirs.
Yes, we all shipped out here for leisure
to create; but Africa's complexities of pleasure
confuse ambition and make truth like lies.
A garrulous snake is at the heart of Paradise.

I Hated Africans

1

The patent soap dispenser
installed last July
worked well, was replenished
once and went dry.

The neat lecturers' houses
are seldom rainproof.
Water runs down my light flex
from a crack in the roof.

Maintenance deal with this
by sending some of the Blacks
at the end of the rainy season
to paint over the cracks.

2

There's a mango tree on the main road
laden with green fruit
they never allow to ripen.
Kids and labourers loot

their own harvest. I hated
Africans annually . . .
the sweet smell of mangoes
bitten and thrown away.

My people invested
in Africa. They knew how to wait
for profits and send charity
too little and too late.

African Bonfire

Guy Fawkes day is for fun. It isn't holy.
We, at the Staff Club after sundown, sat
chatting and idly boozing, ogling at
a straw man being burnt and writhing slowly.

Out of that fine blaze flames in abstract curves
leapt up and turned to sparks, just like most flame;
but we were squirming. It was not the same
old ritual. Every ritual killing deserves

attention, more than to sit around and gloat.
These Hausas tasted blood a month ago,
hacked down my neighbour with a garden hoe.
That savagery made them more remote.

This savagery we celebrate makes ties.
We keep our mouths shut and avoid their eyes.

Marvin the Painter

After a year on the damned campus
I moved in to town.
The staff's so bloody bourgeois
they got me down.
Their club and their film society
and their Dixieland band,
drinks and small-chop parties . . .
Why leave England?
When June went off with Krassner
I took in Maude.
I reckon I'll get some work done
here on my tod.

I come across my colleagues
out dancing in a crowd
or alone, drunk and nervous,
out for a cheap ride,
as for instance our campus poet,
pissed as a newt,
clowning around with a gorgeous
Fulani prostitute.
Maude thought we ought to save him
a night in the stews,
so they both came back to our house
for a clean bed and booze.

On Secondment

Lips crack, throats ache, the wind's so dry
(Oh those Van Goghs in Amsterdam!).
'Cheap. Cheap,' the desperate traders cry.
Buy up ibejis, friend, and scram.

When tulip trees raise cups of blood
(Those village trees in central France!)
the laterite roads are dark red mud,
and Tony's full at the Leavers' Dance.

The sudden wind makes curtains rise
(The taste of cheap red Spanish wine).
Students all night revise, revise.
I am well done with teaching mine.

The lecturers queue at KLM
(Oh, misty days, coal fires and stout!).
All my lads failed. Hard luck on them.
We'll mercifully soon be out.

The Verandah. Zaria.

Stylish in every detail of legs and wings,
evolved like us from mud, they turn
in quick graceful controlled rings
around my reading candle and burn.

Light engineering in each limb,
intricacies of fold and skirt,
God's plenty, his ingenious whim.
Next day we sweep them into heaps like dirt.

The Verandah. Zaria. 2

Boredom, exasperation, the awful heat.
I crunched to death under my shod feet
beetles that swarmed on my verandah, then stared
at cracked frames smeared on cement, scared
of brutality and wantonness, released in me,
releasing the world's wanton brutality.

Guilt was inventing judgement. Above me towered
a god's equivalent of boots. I cowered
for a hard second, an eternity;
but I survived and God faded away.

Nomads

Hairstyles, clothes,
utensils are ornate.
Lacking storerooms and shelves
but wealthy in words,
their world is moving,
their customs elaborate,
their saddles finely engraved
and scabbards and sharp swords.

Sheikh Mohammed's Song on the Death of Corfield
(adapted from a translation)

*In 1913 a Dervish tribe wiped out a British camel detachment
led by Richard Corfield.*

You are dead, Corfield. You are out of this world
and terrible was your departure.
Hell is your destination in the other world,
but if God is willing the Faithful will look down
and question you from Heaven.

Answer the Jewels of Heaven.
Say how God tried you. Say:
'From the first day the Dervish attacks
never faltered. Our famous squares were broken.
The clamour of battle broke over us.'

Say: 'The first attack was at mid-morning.
          A bullet from one of their ancient rifles
          struck me.'

Report with what savage adroitness their swords tore you.
Show to our ancestors red holes in flesh from the daggers.
Say how you whined for compassion, you called out, 'Spare me,'
and staring in every hopeless direction your heart was plucked
from its nest. Your eyes were stiff with horror.
Tell them no mercy was granted.
Spear butts, striking your mouth, deformed soft words.
Say:
          'The risks I took, my blunders, cost me my life.'
Say:
          'I had cherished ambitions of spoil and conquest,
          but the men who killed me will hear my screams forever.'

Say:

     'Outbreaks of shouting mocked my departing soul.'

Say:

     'Beasts of prey are nosing my torn flesh.'

We can hear the hyena swallowing fat. Tell them.
Tell how the vultures sucked your veins and tendons.

Say:

     'The defeat was absolute, inexcusable.
     Everyone knows. In the last stand of resistance
     there is always great slaughter.'

Say:'

     'Like a storm the Dervishes come, rumbling and
                                   roaring.'

Nigerian Cattleman's Song
(based on a literal translation)

At Kandi SHE WHO TEASES laid back her horns.
At Sokoto we played tricks on THE ONE WHO ADVANCES ON
ENEMIES,
ha, we gave her the calf of THE ONE WHOSE HORNS SPREAD
BROADLY.
Ha, she mistook it for hers.
Ho. At Kaura Namoda the lazy locals marvelled
at THE ONE WITH WHITE BLAZES ON HER FOREHEAD,
ho, for she went skipping among them
light on her four hooves despite her grandeur.
As we left that village the various herd lowed with one voice.

At Katsina the herd walked proudly. Ayee.
Themselves they killed a marauder.
At Katsina too SHE WHO STANDS OUT ABOVE THE HERD
gave birth
and so did SHE WHO GRAZED ON THE RIDGE.
On the road South SHE WHO PREVENTS OTHERS APPROACHING
got friendly with ONE WHOSE HORNS ARE AS STRAIGHT AS
PLANKS.
They showed off their slim bodies together.
They displayed the tips of their horns.

At the great city of Kano the herd danced in unison
and played together in the light rain.

At Zaria death struck and the herd was patient.
They died as the four princes of Kano died,
tricked, locked in the burning tent, pressing together
while walls of flame embraced them.

THE ONE WHO RETURNS HOME WITH PRIDE was groaning
all night.
It was heart's pain for the herdsmen to listen.

The Kaduna people were amazed to observe the herd.
They asked if SHE WHOSE HORNS REACH OVER THE WATER
TROUGHS
and SHE WHOSE HORNS ARE LIKE POLISHED REEDS were
sisters?
Were they daughters of SHE WHOSE HORNS STICK OUT OF
THE BUSHES?
I laughed at them. They will never know these beasts.

These are the daughters of THE LEADER WHO MAKES THE
REGION WONDER.

The idle people of Minna were also curious.
'Why was one cow so friendly with another?
Were both of them of the same mother?'
I answered, 'We who live with cattle
still have imperfect knowledge.
How can they ever be known to you,
the hangers-on of the Europeans?'

The ground was parched here and we turned Eastwards.
We passed through many villages at speed, the cattle
pressing against me like warriors challenging.
The land, burnt and wasted, was a kick in the teeth.

At camp I was pacing up and down all night
at the side of SHE WHO GIVES BLOWS AND BRUISES.
But, oh, when we came to Jos, the ground rising. Ha,
plentiful was the water. Ayee, the herd drank and relaxed,
and all the people there took pleasure in watching.

SHE WHOSE HORNS ARE NOT JUST DECORATION ran all the way,
and the milkers avoided THE RESTLESS ONE.

Oh, slim cows, these have been long days and nights,
such a bitter journey would defeat many a one,
but on Jos plateau your horns
point upward again.